My Mom Is a Carpenter

Relate Addition and Subtraction to Length

Maryann Baker

PowerKiDS
press™

NEW YORK

Published in 2015 by The Rosen Publishing Group, Inc.
29 East 21st Street, New York, NY 10010

Book Design: Mickey Harmon

Photo Credits: Cover (woman), pp. 5, 22 auremar/Shutterstock.com; cover (background) Sergej Razcodovskij/
Shutterstock.com; p. 7 Small Town Studio/Shutterstock.com; p. 9 CHAIWATPHOTOS/Shutterstock.com;
p. 11 wavebreakmedia/Shutterstock.com; p. 13 anson/Shutterstock.com; p. 15 Christian Delbert/Shutterstock.com;
p. 17 Atthapol Saita/Shutterstock.com; p. 19 Ruta Production/Shutterstock.com; p. 21 satit_srihin/Shutterstock.com.

Library of Congress Cataloging-in-Publication Data

Baker, Maryann, author.
My mom is a carpenter : relate addition and subtraction to length / Maryann Baker.
    pages cm. — (Math masters. Measurement and data)
Includes index.
ISBN 978-1-4777-4813-8 (pbk.)
ISBN 978-1-4777-4814-5 (6-pack)
ISBN 978-1-4777-6405-3 (library binding)
1. Arithmetic—Juvenile literature. 2. Measurement—Juvenile literature. 3. Carpentry—Mathematics—Juvenile literature.
I. Title.
QA115.B85 2015
513—dc23
                                        2013046664
Manufactured in the United States of America

CPSIA Compliance Information: Batch #WS15RC: For further information contact Rosen Publishing, New York, New York at 1-800-237-9932.

Contents

A Carpenter's Job

My mom has a very cool job. She's a carpenter! Carpenters build and fix things made from wood and other **materials**. Some carpenters work on big **projects**, such as **constructing** large buildings. Others help build homes, fix wooden objects, or make tables and chairs.

My mom helps build and fix things for people's homes. She's very good at her job.

My mom uses many different math skills at her job.

At the Lumberyard

My mom visits a lumberyard to get the materials she needs to do her job. This is a place that sells lumber, or wooden boards that are cut to different sizes.

My mom buys 10 feet of lumber from maple trees and 15 feet of lumber from oak trees. By adding 10 feet and 15 feet together, I know she buys 25 feet of lumber altogether.

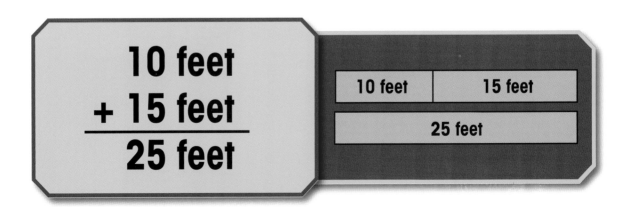

$$\begin{array}{r} 10 \text{ feet} \\ + 15 \text{ feet} \\ \hline 25 \text{ feet} \end{array}$$

10 feet	15 feet
25 feet	

I know that when I add or subtract lengths, I have to remember to include the **unit** of measurement in my answer. When I add 2 lengths measured in feet together, my answer needs to be in feet, too.

Making a Table

My mom uses some of the lumber she bought at the lumberyard to make a table. She has a piece of oak lumber that's 15 feet long. She cuts 6 feet of it off with a saw. How much oak is left for her to use for other projects? I can use a drawing to show how many feet are left.

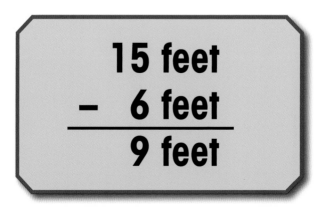

$$15 \text{ feet}$$
$$- \ 6 \text{ feet}$$
$$9 \text{ feet}$$

15 feet

6 feet | **9 feet**

If I draw a line showing 15 feet and cross out 6 feet, I can see that there are 9 feet of oak lumber left.

Building Cabinets

My mom also builds cabinets, which are pieces of **furniture** with drawers or **shelves** used to hold objects. The first parts of a cabinet my mom builds are the shelves.

My mom uses a piece of wood that's 26 inches long to build 2 shelves, and 1 of the shelves is 13 inches long. How long is the other shelf? I can use a question mark to stand for the unknown length.

I subtract the length that I know from the total length. When I subtract 13 inches from 26 inches, I get 13 inches. That's how long the second shelf is.

13 inches
+ ? inches
─────────
26 inches

26 inches
− 13 inches
─────────
13 inches

? = 13 inches

11

Next, my mom builds doors for the cabinet. The cabinet she's building has 2 doors. Each door is made from a piece of wood that's 34 inches long.

I use addition to find out how much wood she uses altogether. I also make sure to show my answer using the correct unit of measurement.

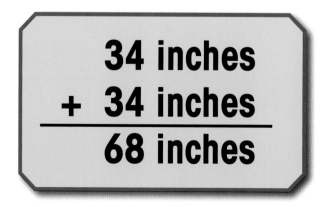

$$34 \text{ inches}$$
$$+\ 34 \text{ inches}$$
$$68 \text{ inches}$$

34 inches   **34 inches**

When I add 34 inches and 34 inches, I get 68 inches.
That's how much wood my mom uses to make
the cabinet doors.

A New House

Sometimes my mom helps other carpenters work on larger projects, such as building a new house. My mom is good at building staircases, so she's building 2 of them for a new house in our town.

It takes a lot of wood to build a staircase. She uses 25 feet of wood for 1 staircase and 41 feet for the other. How much wood does she use altogether?

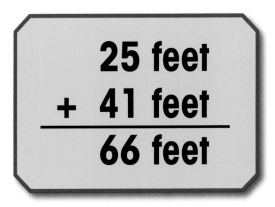

$$\begin{array}{r} 25 \text{ feet} \\ + \ 41 \text{ feet} \\ \hline 66 \text{ feet} \end{array}$$

Carpenters are just 1 kind of construction worker. Many different kinds of construction workers come together to build a new house.

My mom builds furniture for the new house, too. She's building a big bookcase for 1 of the bedrooms. She uses a piece of wood that's 3 meters long for the sides of the bookcase and another piece that's 1 meter long for the top of the bookcase. How much wood does she use altogether?

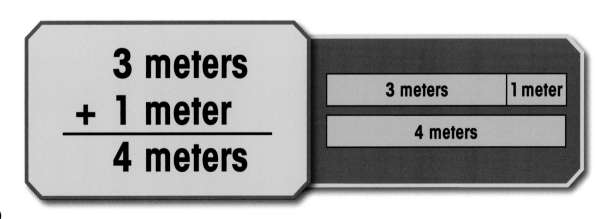

$$\begin{array}{r} 3 \text{ meters} \\ + \ 1 \text{ meter} \\ \hline 4 \text{ meters} \end{array}$$

3 meters	1 meter
4 meters	

Inches and feet are units of measurement called U.S. standard units. A meter is a unit from a system of measurement called the metric system.

17

Working with My Mom

My mom uses her skills as a carpenter to help me build a tree house in our backyard. In 1 weekend, we use 100 inches of wood altogether. If we use 70 inches of wood on Saturday, how many inches do we use on Sunday?

I can use subtraction to help me find the unknown number. What do you get when you subtract 70 from 100?

If an addition problem has an unknown number in the middle, I know I can use subtraction to find what that number is.

70 inches
+ ? inches
—————————
100 inches

100 inches
− 70 inches
—————————
? inches

My mom and I build a birdhouse together, too. She teaches me how to measure wood using another metric unit called a centimeter, which is much smaller than a meter.

We use 76 centimeters of wood for the walls of the birdhouse and 21 centimeters for the roof. How many centimeters of wood do we use altogether?

76 centimeters
+ 21 centimeters
? centimeters

My mom helps me use the tools we need to make the birdhouse. She makes sure I'm using the saw and other tools safely.

My mom works very hard on all her construction projects—from the biggest houses to the smallest tables and chairs. I feel proud to have a mom who works so hard at such a cool job. I also feel happy to have a mom who's teaching me so much about being a carpenter. I love building things with her!

Building things is a fun way to use math in the real world.

Glossary

construct (kuhn-STRUHKT) To build something by putting together a number of parts.

furniture (FUR-nih-chur) Movable things used to make a room ready for use.

material (muh-TIHR-ee-uhl) Something from which something else can be made.

project (PRAH-jehkt) A task.

shelf (SHELF) Something flat and raised that's used to hold objects.

unit (YOO-nuht) A standard amount by which things are measured.

Index

Due to the changing nature of Internet links, The Rosen Publishing Group, Inc., has developed an online list of websites related to the subject of this book. This site is updated regularly. Please use this link to access the list: www.powerkidslinks.com/mm/mad/mmc